We All Belong

We All Belong

Anita M. Hessenauer

RESOURCE *Publications* • Eugene, Oregon

WE ALL BELONG

Copyright © 2021 Anita M. Hessenauer. All rights reserved. Except for brief quotations in critical publications or reviews, no part of this book may be reproduced in any manner without prior written permission from the publisher. Write: Permissions, Wipf and Stock Publishers, 199 W. 8th Ave., Suite 3, Eugene, OR 97401.

Resource Publications
An Imprint of Wipf and Stock Publishers
199 W. 8th Ave., Suite 3
Eugene, OR 97401

www.wipfandstock.com

PAPERBACK ISBN: 978-1-6667-0012-1
HARDCOVER ISBN: 978-1-6667-0013-8
EBOOK ISBN: 978-1-6667-0014-5

05/14/21

In remembrance
of
Laika
and
for
Riley
Whose purity of heart
Continues to inspire me

Contents

Introduction · ix

Jewels of Great Price · 1
Tabula Rasa · 4
Without You . . . · 9
Presence · 13
The Wait · 16
Martyred Paths · 19
A Simple Glance · 21
Unlatched · 23
Cochlea · 25
Life . . . Goes On · 28
Symphony · 31
Topography · 34
Vision · 36
Let Love Enter In . . . · 38
Togetherness · 40
Roots · 42
Hold On- · 43
Hijra · 45
Hear the Silent Cries · 48
Venom · 51
Daily Deaths · 55
If Life Was Only . . . · 57
What Will You Do with This Hurt? · 59

Celebration of the worth and value of every life.

In the tortuous maze of life, it is so easy to miss a turn, to step off the well paved path . . . to lie in the mire of doubt, questioning one's self-worth. The entire gamut of elements that assail us along our journey, tearing our lives asunder by guilt and shame, slicing our hearts with the dagger of rejection and exclusion, the burden of sociological barriers, everything that encompasses the cruelty of the world striking its severe blows is offered to our Maker. We wait for acceptance and for the transformation of our deepest wounds and hurts. Our hearts cry out with the longing that a greater good may be born out of this pain, guilt and suffering. The natural world alongside which we live, is in many instances, the bright patchwork quilt that surprises, with lessons to be learned, paths to be followed.

I offer this poetic bouquet to our Creator who holds all of creation without exception, in the divine embrace. The poems in this collection are but a minute reflection of the infinite love of the Maker for humanity-for you and for me. I stand in awe of this grace filled parachute which extends an unconditional welcome to all in this created order.

There is worth
There is value
In every life
Despair
Is drowned
In the seas
of
Hope
and
Love

The Portal
Flung Open
To
Every Mind and Heart

Jewels of Great Price

Bejeweled miracle
Audubon's pearl of great price.
Enter the avian microcosm
Of filigreed finery
Antithesis of mere plumage
Plunging deeper than the eye can see
Or the mind fathom
Brush strokes
In flight
Mesmerizing
Drinking deeply
Of the treasures
Of the red petunias
Whose wide-open faces smile
The blossoms raising their hands
In reverent offering
Laying their gifts on the altar
The pungent aroma
Rising like incense.
The ambrosia flows unstemmed
A gift given freely
To feed and strengthen another.
Take and drink

No question of hoarding
The eternal circle
Of giving without cost.
The laryngeal cavity satiated
Readies itself to nourish the other
Fills the open throats of famished,
helpless babes

Tucked away in the foliage.
I am my brother's keeper -
The refrain plays
like a broken record
Repeating itself
In the subliminal mind
While the slogan "each for himself"
Screeches
Ever more strident
My conscience gnaws at me
I am over swept by guilt
A slap of the wing
A digging of talons.

The panoply of crows, grackles
And starlings dominate
Stake their territory
Yet the house sparrows, finches and songbirds
Get their fill
In the bouillabaisse of inclusion
A motley crowd.

The blue jay stands guard
His piercing cries
Warning of predatory danger
Saves lives
Silence enwraps the feeders.
The crows in their chivalrous armor
Force the Cooper's to a shameful retreat.

Who is our sentinel?
Who will stem the tide of hate and persecution?
The blurred faces outlined
in the patchwork of flora and foliage
Sharpen
Stretch out their hands with deafening cries.
The frantic swaying of the supple birch
Is none other than the hunger of a lost humanity

Longing to be included
In the melting pot of creation
Can I be the bees' balm?
The salve
Healing the bleeding heart?
The voice
That welcomes into the fragrant patch
The bodies
Drooping, breaking
Under
The weight
Of rejection
Imprisoned
In the starkly cold bramble
Overrun by ivy?
The lethal serum
Seeping steadily into the veins.
The cries intensify
I gesture to the figures
"Come step into the circle
We are all blood relatives"
There is no stranger
There is no alien
The birch extends its lissome members
Dips down
Stirs the potpourri of unity
Melding into the pot of love

Tabula Rasa

Lancelot
In
Chivalrous
Armor
Grimier
Than
A Chimney Sweep
Dripping
Coated
Layered
Ossified
Mummified.
Grime
Filth
Mud
Embedded
In
Every
Crevice.
Toenails
Feast
For
Fungi,
Harder
Than
Cement.
Heart
Encased
In
Asphalt.
Guilt Ridden

Imposter
Without
Remorse.

I
Present
Myself
Without
A plea
Mute . . .
I dare not
Look him
In the eye
I hold my breath . . .
What comes next?

Tingles running
Down the spine
Frozen.
Stooping down
He
Holds
My
Callused
Feet
Gently
Patiently
Takes
His
Time
Scrubs
Away
Years
Of
Grime
And
Dissimulation
Unwraps

The
Burial cloths.
Knots
Woven
Lianas
Of
The
Amazon
Torn
Down
A clearing.
The past
Embedded
In concrete
Longing
to
Evaporate
Into
The
Atmosphere
Piled
Into
A
Neat
Mound
Set Aside
Forgotten.
Passage
Hewn
Bridge
Formed
I
Walk
On
The
Path
Of
Love

And
Compassion

Get down
On your knees
On all fours
Crawl
Into
The
Nook
And
Crannies
You
Dared
Not
Approach
Turned
Your
Back On.
The
Lifeless
Barren
Spaces
Which
Made
You
Take
To your heels.

Enter
Into
The Dark
Tunnel
Bury
Yourself
In
The
Depths

Let
Courage
Rise
Overtake
You -
Plunge
Into
The
Entrails
Of
Mankind.
O deep sea diver
Bring
To
The
Surface
The
Long
Lost
Treasure
Shunned
Quashed
Forgotten . . .
If not you
Then who?
Another
Chance
At
Life
Breathable
Filling
The
Lungs
Another
Ray
Of
Hope
To
Come
Out
Clean

Without You . . .

Drowning in the seas of anxiety
Dashed on the rocks of fear
Swallowed by the beast of panic
Prisoner
Trapped in its iron clad jaw.
Carried
Through an endless
Labyrinth
Swept in waves of darkness.
Multiplicity of buoys
Tossed in the tempest
Submerged
Struggling
To stay afloat
Hands flailing
Gasping for survival.

Marooned.
An island
Crawling
Clawing
To safety.
The tree
Only source
Of
Vegetation
Bare branches
Not
A
Blossom.
Swaying

In
The
Gale
Unbroken
Unscathed
Standing tall
Majestic
Adorned
With
Thorns
A
Babul.
Lighthouse
Incessantly
Beaming
Calling out
Penetrating
Piercing
Shafts
Of
Light
Scanning
The
Wreckage
The devastation
Ready
To
Envelop
To
Gather
In
An
Embrace.
I am
A
Clinging
Parasite
Coiled

Reptilian
Wrapped
Around
The
Trunk.
Soothed
Caressed
Cradled
On
A
Bed
Of
Thorns
My
Down
Feathered
Nest
Refusing
To
Separate
From
My
Host.
Feeling
The
Infusion
The
Warmth
Rises
Like
A
Flood
Pouring
Through
The
Sluice
Propagating
Osmosis.

Fragrance
Spreading
Strength
Building
Mounting.
Confidence
Returning
I face
The storm.

Presence

Muddied
Sullied
Waters
Raging
Torrent
Carrying
Humanity
In its
Wake.
One way -
Go
With the flow -
Can not
Change course.
Aquamarine
Gulped down
Ruby red
Afloat
Etched
In
Calcium strokes
Life size
Monolithic
Picassoesque.
Lachrymal
Lachrymose
The battlefield.
Tectonic plates
Shift
Fissure
Opens

Widens
Yawns
Entombed.
Flood gates
Burst
Inundating
Sparing nothing.
Drawing out
A blunt
Perfectly smooth
Fisherman's hook
The skeletal frame
A morass
Buried
Deep
Within
The
Dung heap
The *kachra kundi*.
Cradle the bones
Breathe
The breath
The fire
Of life.
Disease ridden
Body
Languishing
In
Tenebrific
Isolation
Obscurity
Its
Family.
Groping
Grappling
In blindness
Stifled
In barriers

Hemmed
In
By
The
Prison walls.
The echoes
Of
Silence.
Toll
The
Bells
Of
Abandonment.
Belonging
Kinship
Unknown
Absent
To
The
Comprehension.

Muddied
Bloodied
Surge
Locks
Flung
Wide
Uncaged
Sans frontières
Libre
Libération
Awakened
Arisen
Arms
Outstretched
Basking
In
The
Light

The Wait

Hidden Gems
Brought to light
In cataclysmic times.
Baubles thought
Forever lost
Rediscovered
A treasure trove.
The wheelchairs
Lined up against the wall
Proudly display their occupants
Hugging their life's breath.
"Fragile"
"Handle with care"
Stamped in large, bold letters
On every package
The contents -
Camouflaged
Sunken
Buried
In layers
Of frayed throws
In vibrant colors
Giving away
The darkened toes
Nibbled
And
Cold.
The ones who hold
The lucky charm
Fix their expectant gaze
On the door

Yes, the entry
To a world forgotten
Quashed into the haze.
Blossoms spent
On broken stems
Hanging precariously
By a delicate filament.
A silver streak
Gossamer
Suspended
In mid-air
A spun cobweb
Melting
Into
The worn plaid.

Pining
Longing
For the touch -
To touch your hand
Your silky
Velvety palm.
To cradle your almond face
To stroke
And run my fingers through
Your thickly, sheened hair.
I
Hear
The
Laughter
Ringing
In
My ears.
Sensory
Illusions
Playing
Cruel
Tricks.

I stretch out my hand
Grasp -
Thin air
Nothing
To clutch
Nothing to hold on to.
The image
Fades
In and out
A mirage.
"Jean!
You're here!"
"Time
To
Paint my nails!"
The wait -
Time stands still
Like a broken clock
Waiting to be wound.
The glass
Mocks
Jeers
Reflects
The rain
Drop
By
Drop
Watering
A dry
Parched land

Martyred Paths

The newspaper
A printed square
Harboring victuals for the day.
"*Bala*, a *chapati, lasun chutney.*"
Shelter from the crows, ravens, vultures
Vision sharp
Piercing as the killing swords
Scavengers
Mowing down
Nose diving
Talons
Penetrating
Merciless
Drawing blood.
Feet tread
Step
    By
Step
The red dirt
Welcomes the worn soles
Of time.
Helping hands
Cushioning
The
Fatigued calluses
Baked to a crisp
In the oppressive
Kiln.
Bandaging
The gorges
Crisscrossing

The heels
Scattering
Red pearls
Lapped up
Instantaneously
Grain by grain
Into
The sands of gratitude.
Collecting patiently
Growing
Into
The steep mountain
Of
Perseverance
Trudging
Toward
The jagged peaks
Of
Fortitude

A Simple Glance

Beauty and Worth
Reside in all
Reject not
What displeases the eye.
The most delicate
Of creatures
The butterfly
Chooses
As its landing pad
The thistle
Overlooked
By all.
Drinking deeply of the nectar
Enclosed in its blossom
A gem hidden
Within the thorny
Exterior.
Beauty is more
Far more
Than
Skin deep.
See with
The eyes
Of the Heart
A mind
Of Love
That
Transforms
That
Binds.
Golgotha

Blossoms
Flowers
Into
Eden
The
Disfigured
Broken
Beyond
Recognition
Shunned
Scorned -
Our
Salvation

Unlatched

The door opens
Without a creak. Soundlessly . . .
You would never know
If it were not for *Prani's* tail
Thumping against the floor
In regularity
Transitioning into
Fast motion
As with a whine
He runs to greet her.
It's Kamala.
She always enters through the back door
Hair neatly braided, the scent of *mogras* filling the room.
Didn't you just leave the paddy field?
Not a sign, no muddy smear -
An infectious smile, silently stroking the pet.
Silent but efficient.
A soft, gentle breeze moving through the house.
Room after room
Swept clean
The clothesline
Proudly displays
The laundry
Lovingly scrubbed
On the outdoor wash stone.
Ayah and *Dhobi* rolled into one.
Bai Sahib, you love *kobi*
I promised Sonu
The *Batata Vadas* would be hers today.

Aai whispers, "what would we do without Kamala?"
Life walks into the house
Always from behind.
I leave the door unlatched
"Bai Sahib, I will be back this evening."
Flashes a smile.

Cochlea

As a child
I put my ears
Against the wall
It was *Aai*
Calling.
Would
The vibrations
Reveal
Her state of mind?
Exasperation,
Impatience
Cool
Normal
Back to the printed word
Curled cochleariform
Words
Ruminating
Dissolving
Digesting
Dropped in storage

Walking on the beach with *Aaji*
I put my ears to the conch
A universe
In the palm of my hand
Beating
Against
The stillness
Concentration
Of my faculties
Cochlear function

In the absence of physicality
Soothing
Calming
The nerves
Sigh of relief
The voice
Streaming into my ears
"Yes, I'm fine, mom
Will be home soon."
Or
"Everything's okay, dear
Not to worry."

I marvel at my dog's ability
To recognize
Her master's footsteps
Ears cocked
Tail wagging
Thrashing
The tile floor
Identification
By
Sound
Cochlear sharpness

In my inner cell
The dust rises
Cloud of smoke
Dark of night
Voices stilled
Hushed
Not a foot fall
Silence Creeps
Breathes
A feathered touch
Imperceptible
The
Word

Tiptoes
Down
My
Winding stairway
Unannounced by
The maître D
No grand *entrée*
Without fanfare
Sweeps
Me
Up
Into
The banquet
Of
Peace
Waltzing
To
Shalom
Feasting
On mercy.

Life . . . Goes On

The syncopated ripples on the water
Ignites fire in the heart.
Placid waters
Ripples calm.
Egrets
Beacons
In the shade
Of the poplars.

Dreams shattered
Hopes dashed
Crushed
By the rocks
Of hostility
Enmity.
Breath stilled
Stymied forever.

Pulsating undercurrent
Tears
A running stream
Gushing, uncontrolled.
Hands
Lifted to the sky
An ethereal offering?
An ultimate plea
For inner peace?

Her faith
Is strong
She clings

She hangs on. . .
The last thread
Of genealogy
Has been severed.
Gone
Her only son
Cancerous
A body ravaged
Prayers unanswered
Her mind
A fog.
Void
Inconsolable.
Grief rises
Spiraling smoke
Stairway
Of communication.
Vapors scalding
Reducing
To nothingness
The fine mist
On the glassy
Pure
Sanctified waters.

Rocks smoothened
Constant flow
Of water.
Edges rounded
Time ticks
Flows
Purifies
Aerates.
The fog lifts
Eyes

Dark wells
Dry
Parched
A cavalcade
Of Canada Geese
Silent
Motionless
One webbed foot
Held high
Pays tribute
To
The fallen soul.

A crumpled mass
Before her maker
Source of solace
And
Consolation.
Rushes rustle
Willow whispers
Egret wades
Poplars sway
Stillness
Calm
Peace

Symphony

Sparrows chatter
Wings flutter
Water splashes
Washed
Clean
Small bodies
Big hearts
Room for all
In the bath.
Finches, Blue Jays, Crows
All in the mix.
Chant rises
Monks in unison
Gregorian
Incantation
Bells toll
Baby immersed
A new creation
Ready to brave the world
Hands raised
Incense flowing.

Dissonance -
Fire crackles
Explosion of volcano
Obliterates
Not
The glow
Of
Embers.
Within

The light burns
Not readily visible
Well-groomed
Smart accoutrements
Silence.
Ships passing
In
The night
Shun
The
Other.
Not a word shared
Not an acknowledgement
Entrenched
In
Self-absorption
Center of axis.
Not
Of
My
Clan
Dismissal -

Sycamores
Wave their branches
Silver hands
Lifted upward.
Fresh faces
Peals of laughter
Floating
Carrying in the wind.
Women in sarees
Sanyasinis
Thumbing
Rudraksha malas
Heart uplifted
Serene

Faces
At peace.
Gate
Thrown
Wide open
To
The skies

Topography

You say you don't remember the day
The light led you down the narrow asphalt path
Urging you, nudging your chair
To turn into that wide driveway.
You say you don't remember that Fall day
When the wind gently caressed your face
Instilled in you the courage
Lent you the confidence
Put the words into your mouth -
This was the day that would shape your future
Give you new life
That you could live again
But you say you don't remember
The memory lost in the fog
In the cloud of spray
Killing the cells
Dropping like mosquitoes
Felled by the fogging.
That day you were atop the mountain
Risen to the heights like a helium balloon
Light and airy -
No fear of bursting
Sure to come down safely, securely
In one piece.
All together
As you had never before -
Into empathetic hands readied to catch you
In their parachute
Blooming like the mums
In variegated autumn colors
The bright-eyed girl wanted to give

Her cherished grandmother.
It was the light that carried you
Lifted you out of the dark valleys
Pulled you out of the rushing current
On to dry land.
Yet . . .
You don't remember
You call it a fluke
You say you're tired
You've had enough . . .
Enough of being pulled
Into the mire
The marsh
Where unlike the egret
And
The blue heron
That gracefully
Alight
Into the clear blue sky
Your feet are stuck
Encased in cement
Dragging you deeper
Underwater.
Yet . . .
Right beside you
Swimming
Among the plankton
The light follows you
A twin.
Carries you to the reef
Sets you gently ashore.

                            The door slams
                     You refuse to remember . . .

Vision

The field of poppies and wildflowers
The stately horses with their erect riders
Docile
Feeding on sugar cubes
From outstretched hands
Moving with noble gait
Through the tall grasses
Staying on course
Not missing a beat
Creatures of perfect circuit.
This is what you see
Through the clear glass panes
Overlooking the prairie
Day after day
Taking on creative turns and jumps
As varied as the jodhpurs and breeches
The equestrian coat and crop
Of the rider
With auburn hair
Neatly tucked under the shiny black helmet.
Your mind
Bright and crisp
As the morning air
Inhales the love
Between the young rider
And
her beloved mare.
Your movements are restricted
You're confined to your chair
You make the effort, painful as it may be
To wave, to smile

Gestures welling up from the depths of your heart
As the rider goes by
Day after day.
You don't see monotony
Boredom is not an ally.
When frustration
Begins to spin its web
You break through with a clean tear
You're far from being a fan
Of its noxious charm,
Refusing to have your hands tied
Or your head bowed down.
Instead, transported to the far-flung corners of the world
Ravaged by poverty, hunger, disease . . . death
You exhale the sweet incense of gratitude
For the gift of vision passing by your front door
Day after day.

Let Love Enter In . . .

Love is in the air
All around you
Waiting
Crying out
Longing
To be received.
Let Love enter in . . .
Bare your heart
Unplug your ears
See . . .
Love's outstretched hand
Steadying you
Whispering
Words
Of
Comfort
Of consolation
Accompanying you
Carrying your burden
Bearing your frustration.
That is LOVE.
Open wide
Your doors
Allow yourself
To be lifted
Enveloped
Consoled
In the arms
Of
Love

Giving up
Calling it quits
Has no place
In the domain of Love.
There are no quick fixes
No immediate "cures"
With the snap of fingers.
Just band aids
For the moment.
Nothing
That's lasting
Nothing that endures.
Perseverance
Moving forward
Surrendering
Is the key.
Place yourself
In the arms of Love.
Let Love
Carry you
Take care of you.
All will be well
In Love's time.

Togetherness

Remember the days
The years gone by.
Be not saddened
Be filled with joy.

This is you
This is me
This is us
Bound together
Walking
In the legacy
Of togetherness.

Building up
Not tearing down
Supporting
Lifting up
Restoring dignity
Positivity
No room for negativity.

Strength in unison
No exclusion
Leaning on the other
Infusion of strength.

Comfort
In the midst of pain
Sharing the grief, the hurt.
Encouragement
Propelling forward

Civilization
Of compassion
Unity
In diversity
Strength to greater strength
A universe
Of
Togetherness

Roots

Radix, radical
Digging deep
Traveling far
Into the depths
Of the humus.
The earth cooperates,
Yielding its treasures
Without restraint, without avarice
Generosity personified.
Branching into uncharted waters
Spreading their fingers,
A lattice strong, secure, productive.
Foliage heavy laden, summer ripened,
Multiform, variegated.
Multidimensional,
Clarity yet opacity,
Shielding not revealing
Baring subtlety.
Lava effusive, carrying gifts numerous,
Buttresses stretching grateful hands,
As their message echoes in the wind -
Gratitude
Love
For well-watered roots.

Hold On -

Hold on -
To the luminaries
Shimmering on the water.
A prismatic burst
A thousand candles
Flickering diadems
Dancing
On tiptoes
Cajoling
Sweeping up
The mallards
In waltz steps
Showing off the ballerinas
In their billowing skirts
Of
Silk tulle
Stepping with grace
Yes, stepping forward
Head held high
Sprinkling a thousand blessings
To be held
In the palm of the heart.
Chiaroscuro.
Myriad particles
Diasporic dust
Accentuating
The halo
Around the finely sculpted
Wood ducks
Quintessential light.
Twilight glistens

On luminescent pearls
Ornate orbs of refulgence
Pride of the poplars
The Great Egrets
Heads nestled
In serene confidence
Into the brow of mother's shoulder
Overtaking night
Reaching for the dawn
Embracing another sunrise.

Hijra

Shrieks of laughter,
Hooting calls,
The streets ring out
With the uproar
Of adults and children alike.
The stray dogs will not be left out.
Bedlam.
The clanging of bells
The din of tambourines
Call the villagers
Into the mud beaten roadway.
The crowd roars
As the stranger appears
Into full view.
The stranger in motley attire
Face heavily made up
Is propelled into the center,
The center of the show ring.
A microcosm.
Little ones pull and tug at the
Multicolored skirt,
Gaudy, blinding the eye
In the summer heat.
Tattered at the ends
Trailing in the dirt.

The stranger laughs
Emitting a hybrid sound.
The highs and lows
Send the crowd
Roaring,

Dancing,
Circling the
Strange figure.
The bells on the feet jingle wildly
As the dancer whirls and twirls
On blistered feet,
Hair flowing freely
In the wind.
Kohl rimmed eyes gleam
Beneath bushy eyebrows.
Lips bright red,
Flashes of stained teeth.
Painted nails
Coy glances
Movements of the head
Synchronize with
A staccato beat.

Coins hit the worn stainless pot
With a clang.
Is this the Pied Piper of Hamelin?
Hypnotizing
With melodic song and dance?
Listen!
Hear the scoffing
See the smirking faces
On one and all alike.
Fingers waggling
Distinct name calling -
Hijra! Hijra!
There's no stopping.
The feet step up their beat
A veritable feat,
Kicking up the red dirt
Forming a cloud of dust
Fodder for the *goondas*
Prime target
Of every *chokra* boy.

The crowd is raucous,
Insults flow,
The mockery grows.

A stray tear
Making its way
Down the visage,
Streaking the
Painted mask,
Falling silently
To the ground
Mingling with the dust
Tells the story -
Outcast
Mendicant
Object of mockery
Butt of crude jokes
Humiliating existence
All to eke out a meager living.

The stranger
Turns back.
The blistered
Callused feet
retrace their steps
To an empty
Cold hut
On the margins
Of civilization
Only to be welcomed
By companions
ever so faithful
Eternally loyal
Closer than a shadow -
Loneliness
Sadness
Emptiness.

Hear the Silent Cries

Dedicated to children around the world
who are victims of violence

Pools lackluster
Vacant gaze
Empty stare
Lifeless yet piercing
Into the abyss of my heart.

Silence abounding
Devoid of emptiness
Plumbing the depths
Of
Humanity
Weighing enormously.
Writhing, groaning
Bodily gymnastics.
Metamorphosis.

Longing, hoping
Wracked in pain.
Helpless
Resignation.
You brought me
Into this world
In your arms
I took shelter
The perfect refuge.
My sky was always blue
The plains in which I skipped
And danced with steps so lithe
A lush green.

The air resounding with peals of laughter
Zenith of lightness
Joy.

All expectancy
Turned to darkness
Somber, stifling
Oppressive
Murderous.
Stilling the Innocents
Annihilating
Decimating
Exterminating
The very breath.

Life invaluable
Ego overshadows
At what price?
To what lengths?
Distinctions man made
Tear asunder.
Blood coursing through the veins
Is the very same color.
A core hardened
Vision blinded
The fire rages
The bodies enflamed
Innocence silenced.

Hold not your hands
Behind your back
Be not tongue tied.
Let your voice
Ring out with vehemence
Stop not
Until every silent cry
Be heard
Every life

Picked up
Put back together
Soothed
Caressed
Loved.
End the massacre.

Venom

Inspired by the heroin addict I saw panhandling regularly on a busy street corner

King Cobra
Beloved
Forever privileged pet.
Palatial abode.
The snake charmer
Overindulgent
Fattens and milks
A continuum.
No repose
Hibernation?
None.
Appetite voracious
The reptilian tongue
Seldom satiated
Forever thirsting
Forever foraging
Aggressively fanning
Its hooded crown.
Ravenous monster
Spreading its tentacles
Igniting the fire
Gluttonous tongue
Horrific entrapment
Merciless engulfment
Total asphyxiation.

Insomniac
No longer concealed
Constantly mobilized

Fully armed
Domineering monarch
Crushing the structure
Into morass.
Skeletal frame
Eyes hollowed
Numbed brain.
Powerlessness
Helplessness
Thirst unquenched
Wasting away
Into nothingness.
In a stupor
Totally oblivious.

The hood is fanned
Holding itself majestically.
Hypnotist
In control
But
Not
forever.
A turn of events.
The wrestling begins
Struggles ensue
In the arena.
Hood has the upper hand
Hood is suppressed
Ad infinitum . . .
Keep it underground
Hear the sizzling
Do not let it spew
Shut the lid tightly.
A step forward
Out of its domain
Regression
Stagnation
Hungering

Thirsting
Craving . . .
Status quo.
Volcanic eruption
Angelic mediation
Never to let go.
Stubborn persistence
Minute
Yet forward progression.
The circumference is enlarged
Sunshine penetrates
Pierces the grime
Creates a dent.
The rays are lengthened
Grow deeper
Osmosis.
Somnambulist
No.
Reality
Here to stay.

Wake up
Shake yourself clean
Walk out of this never ending
Dream
A nightmare.
The mist has lifted

The fog has cleared.
You are no longer a shadow.
Steady yourself
Hold on
To the outstretched
hand -
Never let go.
Your life has value
Not to be thrown away

Akin to a tattered coat
Or well-worn shoes.
Follow the hand
The mesmerizing look
You're given a million chances
Jump into the inviting pool.
Enter the deep
Touch the depths
Rise to the surface
Breathe free.
Chameleon
Colors dappled
Hues transformed
Trust
Hope
Live again.

Daily Deaths

A continuum of internal foray: disappointments, disillusionment
Strung together like clothes hung out to dry.
The clothes pins- blue, green, yellow.
Tricolor
Predictable
Never changing
Never reversed.
The all too familiar paradigm
Patterns the day, repeats itself,
Begins all over again.
Sisyphus pushing his rock up the steep mountain
Only to have it roll down again.
The tie dye, once vibrant
Now washed out.
Stained, soiled, scrubbed on the wash stone
Beaten to a pulp
Wrung out
The heartbeat lost.

Impatience gallops like a runaway colt
Wild, untamed, nostrils flared
Whinnying to a fever pitch
Stomping its hoofs
In its powerlessness.
Frustration gnaws,
An impetuous toddler
In the throes of a tantrum
The toy car blown
To smithereens
The walls sporting their food art.

Spiraling into the doldrums
One way.
No exit.
No ladder dropped
No foothold
No way out.
No ingenuity of mind
No strategizing
Will produce the rope,
Or part the waters,
An escape to firm ground.
In the bog of panic
In the sinking sands
Pushed to the limit

Isn't it time to make a change?
To rearrange the clothes pins
To retain the vibrancy of the print?
Isn't it the moment to break out
Of myself?
To no longer bask in the sweet fragrance of self-reliance?
To unmask the dazzling blooms of pride and arrogance
The ripe blossoms of individualism
That tantalize
And snap me up
A fly on the tongue
Of the spider lily?

I am not the brightest diadem
Lighting up the skies
Nor the axis of rotation
Or the gravitational force.
Impossible to do it on my own.
It's the moment of reckoning -
A total awakening.
I add the vital pin to the clothesline

If Life Was Only...

If life was only a gigantic hug, holding us tight
In its warm, soothing embrace
A purring cat, a cuddly puppy, the fluffiest of bunnies.
If life only offered cake and ice cream in a sugar cone
If our days were dotted only by soft kisses, gentle words,
sweet nothings whispered in the ear
If everyone who crossed our path always wore a smile,
grinning from ear to ear
Politeness,
Love personified.
If our televisions and social media
only portrayed a world
of good neighbors,
the ideal of
Mr. Roger's neighborhood
A happy, cheerful humanity
Alas, where would we be?
What would we become as humans?
Devoid of all humanity...
The words, the qualities we cherish in each other
The empathy to stand
In another's hurting shoes
Torn from the deep wound engraved on the heart.
The compassion to suffer with the one in pain
Wracked with sorrow.
A silent presence accompanying another
Lost in grief.
Acts of kindness pouring out from the depths of souls
Kindreds linked together, walking the common road strewn with thorns
Incendiary speech fueled by the raw gasoline of hatred.

Appreciation, gratitude- words and acts forgotten, lost, buried.
Never discovered.
A world enveloped in smugness, a population self-absorbed.
Hearts turned cold, frigid slabs on gravestones.

It is only because of the darkness that slaps us in the face
The darts that pierce our core
That we awaken . . .
Realize we're being torn to shreds
That we cling to the welcome rays of light.
It is only because of injustice that we fight for rights.
It is only because we drink the bitter hyssop
That we savor the sweetness of love
Bubbling up from the heart.
In the absence of night, there would be no day
Without the sunset, not another sunrise.

What will you do with this Hurt?

She whispers
Her words barely audible- Where
does it hurt?
Bandages my heart
Nurses my wound.
A dull pain at first
Sizzling
Rising
O so imperceptibly
Irradiating discomfort
Far reaching ripples.
The shrapnel lodged in the deep
Before the bleeding.
She stirs the tea leaves
With measured strokes
Fighting
the
Black ants struggling chaotically
In the steaming geyser
Daring to strike
Let loose the metal
Fiery vapors
Scalded
Charred
Razed to the ground
Wipe-out.
Must bleed to feed
That's the maxim
Borne out of sword
Out of trigger
Unstoppable.

Ghost towns
Ineffectual specters wandering aimlessly
No phoenix rising majestically
From its ashes.

Apartheid
The monochromatic dagger
Wielded freely
Into unfathomable depths.
Brown rat
Scum of the earth
Reverberating in my ears,
Innards emptied
Blown to bits.
Left to decide . . .
To make a choice.
I pick myself up
Stand erect
Reject the ditch
Where they would rather see me.
The crimson river
Brims over
The hue intensifies
Blazes
Churns
Curdled like spoiled milk.
No dilution
No blends.
I wade through the subcutaneous marsh
Lay the machete down
Place it back into its sheath.
The scab forms
Nourishes its thorns
Into a barbed wire fence.
Digs its roots
Into the nucleus of my soul
Buttresses my heart.

She whispers, do not walk the road of nothingness
  It's the skeleton that waves
  Its knobbly bones
  Into the void.

  Where does it hurt?
  How intense the pain?
  I ruminate over her words
   Seared into my ticker tape.
   Collect your suffering drop by drop.
   Fill the vials, one by one
Store them in your innermost chamber.
Infinitely more precious than the Kohinoor diamond
In the royal crown.
  Hold your hurt close
  Let it not slip away
    Or pass through the sieve
Wasted
Gone forever
  The overflow from a gushing drain.
  Hold on to the pain
  Rise up over the hurt
  Let it morph into wholeness
Believe that you're wonderfully made.
  A heart fragmented
  Blown to smithereens
Is none other than your armor of strength
  Nurture your hurt
    With the tender love for a child
  Until it becomes you
  Welded into your sinews.
And when you can bear the pain no more
  When the hurt is raw
Exposed
No gauze.
  When the fire rages
  And the volcano erupts
Hear the voice whisper
What will you do with this hurt?
    Where will you take this pain?

www.ingramcontent.com/pod-product-compliance
Lightning Source LLC
Chambersburg PA
CBHW061510040426
42450CB00008B/1549